Stop Overthinking
Break the Cycle. Stop Negative Spirals and
Unlock the Power of Your Mind

Rudolf Moore

Copyright 2023 – Rudolf Moore © All rights reserved.

The content contained within this book may not be reproduced, duplicated, or transmitted without direct written permission from the author or the publisher. Under no circumstances will any blame or legal responsibility be held against the publisher, or author, for any damages, reparation, or monetary loss due to the information contained within this book. Either directly or indirectly.

Legal Notice:

This book is copyright protected. This book is only for personal use. You cannot amend, distribute, sell, use, quote or paraphrase any part, or the content within this book, without the consent of the author or publisher.

Table of Content

Author 7

Introduction 10

    Why Do We Think Too Much? 17

Support my Work 27

Recognize useless Thoughts 28

    What's Positive Thinking? 29

    What's Productive Thinking? 33

    What Is Persistent Thinking? 36

How to stop dwelling on negative thoughts 40

    Practical Strategies for Managing Persistent Thinking ... 42

    Management of anxiety and panic 45

    Meditation 47

Support my Work 53

Gratitude and appreciation 54

    How To Reduce Stress 56

    How To Reduce Overthinking 61

Improve Sleep 67

    Sleep Hygiene 68

- Relaxation Techniques for Sleep 69
- Addressing Sleep Disorders 70
- How to reduce Nighttime thinking 71

Support my Work 75

Time Management 76
- Organize To Reduce Stress 83
  - Prioritize your tasks. 83
  - Create a schedule. 84
  - Use a planner or calendar. 86
  - Declutter your spaces. 88
  - Practice Time Management 89
  - Set Boundaries 91

How to Create a Positive Mindset 97
- Boosts Confidence 98
- Increases Productivity 98
- Enhances Relationships 98
- Promotes Overall Well-Being 98

Cultivating Gratitude and Appreciation 99
- Keep a Gratitude Journal 99

Practice Mindfulness 100

Express Gratitude to Others 100

Reframe Negative Experiences 101

Focus on Abundance 101

Building Resilience and Emotional Intelligence 102

Practice Self-Care 102

Build a Support System 103

Learn from Mistakes 103

Develop Emotional Awareness 103

Practice Mindfulness 104

Reframing Negative Thoughts and Beliefs 104

Identify Negative Thoughts and Beliefs 105

Reframe Negative Thoughts and Beliefs 105

Practice Positive Self-Talk 106

Practice Gratitude 106

Challenge Negative Thoughts 107

Reframe Negative Thoughts 107

Use Positive Affirmations 108

Visualize Positive Outcomes 108

    Surround Yourself with Positive People 108

    Practice Mindfulness 109

Conclusion 110

Support my Work 113

Author

Hello, I'm Rudolf. A few years back, I was in a tough spot. I was stuck in a life that wasn't fulfilling, with personal and professional problems that seemed insurmountable. So, I was tempted to give up, but I decided not to.

Instead, I took control of the situation and started looking for a solution to my problems. I read many books, attended international and niche courses and seminars, and put into practice all the techniques I learned. It wasn't easy, but I kept believing that finding a solution was possible.

Over time, I noticed a change in myself. It was like I was a tree that had finally found the correct roots to grow strong and healthy. My relationships improved, I found a job that I was genuinely passionate about, and I started living with more satisfaction and serenity. By cultivating the new habits and perspectives I had acquired, I felt myself becoming more robust and resilient in facing life's challenges.

It wasn't easy, but I stayed determined and didn't give up on myself. I continued to believe that finding a solution was possible and made every effort to find it. The transformation I experienced required commitment, consistency, and patience, but the results were well worth it.

After experiencing such a profound transformation in my own life, I couldn't help but feel a strong desire to share what I had learned with others. I knew that many people were struggling, just as I had been, and could benefit from the strategies and techniques I had discovered.

I felt a sense of responsibility to share what I had learned and offer a hand to others going through tough times. And that's how the idea for this book was born. I wanted to provide a practical guide that could help people transform their lives just as I had changed mine.

I invite you immediately to download the bonus chapter reserved for you directly on your smartphone. Use the camera to frame the QR code on next page.

Through the pages of this book, I hope to inspire and help many others not to give up when they're feeling down, to find solutions to their problems, and to live a more fulfilling and serene life. I know it's not easy, but it's possible, and I'm here to show you how.

Introduction

In today's fast-paced world, it's easy to become consumed by our thoughts. With social media, news outlets, and constant connectivity, we're constantly bombarded with information and stimuli, leading to overwhelming anxiety and stress. As a result, many of us fall into the trap of overthinking, where we obsess over every little detail and analyze every decision we make, often to the point of paralysis.

Overthinking is a mental process where we become preoccupied with a particular thought or idea, often to the point of rumination. It can manifest in various ways, such as over-analyzing past events, worrying excessively about the future, or second-guessing our decisions. Overthinking is a common phenomenon affecting people of all ages and backgrounds, from students to professionals.

While some level of introspection and self-reflection is healthy, overthinking can adversely affect our mental health and well-being. It's been linked to various mental health issues, including anxiety, depression, and obsessive-compulsive disorder (OCD). Overthinking can exacerbate these conditions by increasing the frequency and intensity of negative thoughts, leading to a self-perpetuating cycle of distress.

When we overthink, we tend to dwell on negative thoughts, which can trigger the release of stress hormones like cortisol and adrenaline. These hormones can cause physical symptoms such as headaches, muscle tension, and increased heart rate. Over time, chronic overthinking can lead to more severe health problems, including high blood pressure, heart disease, and a weakened immune system.

Furthermore, overthinking can interfere with our ability to make decisions and act. When caught up in our thoughts, we may become paralyzed by indecision or doubt, leading to missed opportunities and decreased productivity. In some cases, overthinking can even prevent us from pursuing our goals and dreams as we become consumed with fear and self-doubt.

Overthinking can be triggered by various factors, including stress, anxiety, and past trauma. For example, suppose we've experienced a traumatic event. In that case, we may find ourselves constantly replaying it, trying to make sense of it, or finding a solution. Similarly, if we're going through high stress, we may become fixated on our problems and worry excessively about the future.

The adverse effects of overthinking can be significant, leading to increased anxiety and stress, decreased productivity, and general unhappiness. However, the good news is that overthinking is a habit that can be broken, and the benefits of doing so are numerous. By learning how to manage our thoughts and focus on the present moment, we can improve our mental health, reduce stress, and increase our happiness and well-being.

This book aims to provide practical tools and strategies to help you overcome overthinking and lead a more mindful, intentional life. Whether you're struggling with anxiety, stress, or simply feeling overwhelmed by the demands of modern life, this book will help guide you towards a more peaceful, centered way of being.

In the following chapters, we'll explore the science behind overthinking, including how it impacts our mental health and well-being. We'll also examine common triggers that can lead to overthinking, such as stress, anxiety, and past trauma. Finally, armed with this knowledge, we can identify the patterns and behaviors contributing to our overthinking and develop strategies to overcome them.

One of the key strategies we'll explore is mindfulness. Mindfulness is a practice that involves bringing our attention to the present moment without judgment or distraction. By cultivating mindfulness, we can manage our thoughts and emotions more effectively and develop a greater sense of inner calm and well-being.

We'll also explore cognitive-behavioral therapy (CBT), a form of treatment that helps individuals identify and challenge negative thought patterns. By learning to recognize and reframe our negative thoughts, we can break free from the cycle of overthinking and develop a more positive outlook on life.

Another strategy we'll delve into is positive psychology, the scientific study of what makes life worth living. Focusing on our strengths and cultivating positive emotions, we can develop a more resilient mindset and enhance our overall well-being.

Throughout the book, we'll provide practical exercises and techniques to help you implement these strategies daily. By committing to these practices and taking small, consistent steps towards a more mindful, intentional way of being, you can break free from the cycle of overthinking and live a more fulfilling life.

In conclusion, this book is designed to be a comprehensive guide for anyone struggling with overthinking. By providing a deep understanding of the science behind overthinking and exploring a range of practical strategies for overcoming it, we hope to empower readers to take control of their thoughts and emotions and live a more peaceful, centered life.

The problem of overthinking

Overthinking can be a severe problem that affects many people. It is a condition that involves excessive or repetitive thinking, often about negative experiences, or possible future events. While some level of thinking is customary and even necessary, overthinking can lead to stress, anxiety, and other negative consequences. In this chapter, we will explore the problem of overthinking, including its causes, symptoms, and effects on mental health.

Overthinking is a mental condition that involves obsessing over a particular problem, situation, or event. It can be triggered by anxiety, depression, other mental health disorders, and stressful life events such as a breakup, job loss, or financial troubles. Overthinking can also occur due to a personality trait or coping mechanism, such as perfectionism or procrastination.

Symptoms of overthinking can vary, but common signs include excessive worry or rumination, difficulty making decisions, trouble sleeping, and an inability to focus. Overthinking can also cause physical symptoms such as headaches, fatigue, and muscle tension. In severe cases, overthinking can lead to panic attacks or other mental health conditions.

The effects of overthinking on mental health can be significant. For example, overthinking can increase feelings of anxiety and depression, leading to a negative impact on mood and overall quality of life. It can also interfere with relationships, work, and social interactions, making functioning difficult.

Causes of overthinking can be complex and multifactorial. Genetic predisposition, environmental factors, and individual personality traits can all play a role. For example, people with a history of anxiety or depression may be more prone to overthinking. At the same time, those who are perfectionists or tend towards negative thinking may also be at risk.

Treatment for overthinking can involve a variety of strategies, including cognitive-behavioral therapy, mindfulness meditation, and stress reduction techniques. These approaches help individuals identify and challenge negative thought patterns, develop coping skills, and improve overall mental health.

Overthinking is a complex and potentially serious problem that can impact mental health, relationships, and overall quality of life. While some level of thinking is ordinary and necessary, excessive, or repetitive, thinking can lead to stress, anxiety, and other negative consequences. The causes of overthinking are multifactorial and may involve genetics, environmental factors, and individual personality traits. Treatment for overthinking can involve a variety of approaches, including cognitive-behavioral therapy, mindfulness meditation, and stress reduction techniques. Individuals can improve their mental health and overall well-being by understanding the problem of overthinking and seeking appropriate treatment.

Why Do We Think Too Much?

Overthinking, or overthinking, is an expected behavior that can negatively affect mental health and overall well-being. Overthinking can be characterized by excessive or repetitive mental activity, including persistent worry, rumination, and negative thinking. This chapter will explore what it means to overthink, including its physical and emotional effects, and how it can be managed.

Overthinking can have a variety of physical effects on the body. For example, when people engage in excessive thinking, they may experience physical symptoms such as headaches, muscle tension, or fatigue. These symptoms can be caused by activating the body's stress response, which can increase the production of hormones like cortisol and adrenaline.

Overthinking can also affect the quality of sleep. When people engage in excessive thinking, they may have difficulty falling or staying asleep, leading to fatigue, and reduced cognitive function during the day. Poor sleep quality can also increase stress and anxiety, leading to a cycle of rumination and negative thinking.

Overthinking can also have a variety of emotional effects on the individual. For example, when people engage in excessive thinking, they may experience persistent stress, anxiety, or sadness. This can lead to a reduced quality of life, as people may need help engaging in daily activities or socializing with others.

Overthinking can also interfere with decision-making and problem-solving. When people engage in excessive thinking, they may become trapped in a cycle of rumination, making it difficult to make clear-headed decisions or find practical solutions to problems.

There are a variety of causes of overthinking, including environmental factors, individual coping strategies, and mental health conditions.

Environmental factors can contribute to overthinking by increasing feelings of stress and anxiety. For example, a high-pressure work environment or a demanding social situation can lead to increased feelings of stress, leading to increased rumination and negative thinking.

Individual coping strategies can also contribute to overthinking. When people engage in coping strategies that are ineffective or maladaptive, they may inadvertently increase their level of stress and anxiety, leading to more excessive thinking.

For example, avoidance coping strategies, such as avoiding difficult situations or thoughts, can contribute to excessive thinking. On the other hand, people who engage in release coping may avoid problems that make them feel anxious or stressed, leading to a cycle of rumination and negative thinking.

Mental health conditions such as anxiety and depression can also contribute to overthinking. People with mental health conditions may experience persistent stress or sadness, leading to increased rumination and negative thinking.

There are a variety of management strategies that can be used to reduce excessive thinking and manage its effects. Some of these strategies are discussed below.

Mindfulness meditation involves focusing on the present moment without judgment or distraction. Mindfulness meditation can reduce excessive thinking by helping individuals develop a more mindful and accepting attitude toward their thoughts and emotions.

The physical nature of overthinking is complex and involves various brain regions. The prefrontal cortex, for example, is involved in higher-order cognitive functions such as decision-making and problem-solving. On the other hand, the amygdala is involved in emotional processing. It can become overactive in response to stress or anxiety. Overthinking can cause an imbalance between these two regions, leading to a persistent state of rumination and negative thinking.

Excessive thinking can be triggered by various factors, including stressful life events, mental health disorders, and individual coping strategies. For example, when people experience stress, anxiety, or other negative emotions, they may engage in excessive thinking to try to cope with or solve their problems. In this chapter, we will explore some of the triggers of extreme thinking, including their physical and emotional effects, and how they can be managed.

Stressful Life Events:

Stressful life events can be a significant trigger for excessive thinking. These events can be major or minor, including things like a breakup, job loss, financial troubles, or health problems. When people experience a significant stressor, they may engage in excessive thinking to try to cope with the situation.

The physical effects of stress can also contribute to excessive thinking. When people are under pressure, their bodies produce cortisol, a hormone that can affect how the brain processes information. High levels of cortisol can cause an increase in negative thinking and rumination, making it more challenging to turn off or control one's thoughts.

Mental Health Disorders:

Mental health disorders can also be a significant trigger for excessive thinking. Conditions like anxiety, depression, and obsessive-compulsive disorder (OCD) can cause persistent rumination and negative thinking, making it difficult to focus or engage in daily activities.

The physical effects of mental health disorders can also contribute to excessive thinking. For example, people with anxiety may experience physical symptoms like a racing heartbeat or sweaty palms, which can increase feelings of stress and anxiety and contribute to excessive thinking.

Individual Coping Strategies:

Individual coping strategies can also contribute to excessive thinking. When people engage in coping strategies that are ineffective or maladaptive, they may inadvertently increase their level of stress and anxiety, leading to more excessive thinking.

For example, avoidance coping strategies, such as avoiding difficult situations or thoughts, can contribute to excessive thinking. On the other hand, people who engage in release coping may avoid problems that make them feel anxious or stressed, leading to a cycle of rumination and negative thinking.

Another example of an ineffective coping strategy is self-criticism. Self-critical people may engage in excessive thinking to try to solve their problems or avoid negative consequences. However, this strategy can be counterproductive, leading to a cycle of rumination and negative thinking.

Management Strategies:

There are a variety of management strategies that can be used to reduce excessive thinking and manage its triggers. Some of these strategies are discussed below.

Social Support:

Social support can also be effective in reducing excessive thinking. For example, spending time with friends or family, participating in social activities, or joining a support group can provide a sense of connection and belonging, reducing isolation and stress.

Some of the primary triggers of excessive thinking include:

Stressful life events: Major life changes, such as a divorce, illness, or financial difficulties, can trigger overthinking.

Mental health disorders: Anxiety, depression, and other mental health disorders can cause persistent rumination and negative thinking.

Personality traits: Perfectionism, procrastination, and other personality traits can contribute to overthinking.

Environmental factors: High-pressure work environments or social pressure can contribute to overthinking.

Individual differences refer to how people differ regarding their psychological and physiological characteristics. These differences can be influenced by a variety of factors, including genetics, environmental factors, and personal experiences. For example, regarding overthinking, individual differences can play an important role in why some people are more prone to this behavior than others. This chapter will explore individual differences that can contribute to overthinking, including genetic factors, cognitive styles, and personality traits.

Genetic Factors:

Genetic factors can play a role in the development of overthinking, as well as other mental health conditions. For example, studies have found that people with a family history of anxiety or depression may be more likely to experience overthinking themselves. This may be due to the inheritance of specific genes affecting brain chemistry and regulating mood and emotions.

One gene implicated in developing anxiety and overthinking is the serotonin transporter gene (5-HTT). This gene is responsible for producing a protein that regulates the reuptake of serotonin, a neurotransmitter that regulates mood and anxiety. Some studies have found that people who carry a specific variation of the 5-HTT gene may be more prone to anxiety and overthinking.

Another gene linked to overthinking is the catechol-O-methyltransferase (COMT) gene. This gene is involved in the metabolism of dopamine. This neurotransmitter plays a role in motivation, reward, and cognitive function. Some studies have found that people with a particular variation of the COMT gene may be more prone to overthinking and anxiety.

While genetic factors can contribute to overthinking, it is essential to note that genes are not the only factor. Environmental factors, personal experiences, and individual coping strategies can also play a role in the development of overthinking.

Cognitive Styles:

Cognitive styles refer to how individuals process and respond to information. Different mental types can influence how people approach problem-solving, decision-making, and other cognitive tasks. For example, regarding overthinking, cognitive styles can explain why some people are more prone to excessive thinking than others.

One cognitive style that has been associated with overthinking is analytical thinking. Analytical thinking involves breaking down complex problems into smaller components and analyzing each in detail. While analytical review can be helpful in some situations, it can also lead to overthinking and rumination when applied to personal problems or concerns that do not have a clear solution.

In contrast, intuitive thinking involves relying on gut feelings and intuition to make decisions. While intuitive thinking can be less precise than analytical thinking, it can be more effective when there is no clear solution or time is limited. As a result, people more prone to intuitive thinking may be less likely to engage in overthinking.

Another cognitive style that can influence overthinking is attentional control. Attentional control refers to the ability to focus and maintain attention on a task or thought while filtering out distractions. People with poor attentional control may be more prone to overthinking and distraction, as they have difficulty focusing on a particular task or thought.

Personality Traits:

Personality traits can also explain why some people are more prone to overthinking than others. Personality traits are stable patterns of behavior, thought, and emotion that is relatively consistent over time and across different situations. While many personality traits can influence overthinking, some of the most relevant are discussed below.

One personality trait that is associated with overthinking is neuroticism. Neuroticism is a personality trait characterized by anxiety, worry, and a tendency towards negative emotions. People who score high on neuroticism may be more prone to overthinking and rumination, as they tend to dwell on negative thoughts and experiences.

Another personality trait that can influence overthinking is perfectionism. Perfectionism involves a tendency towards setting high standards for oneself and being self-critical when those standards are unmet. Perfectionistic people may be more prone to overthinking and rumination. They constantly strive for an unattainable level of perfection and may dwell on their perceived failures and shortcomings.

Procrastination is another personality trait that can contribute to overthinking. Procrastination involves putting off tasks until the last minute or avoiding them altogether. People prone to procrastination may be more likely to engage in overthinking as they try to avoid the discomfort and anxiety associated with starting a task.

Finally, low self-esteem can also contribute to overthinking. People with low self-esteem may be more prone to negative thinking and self-criticism, leading to a cycle of rumination and self-doubt.

In conclusion, individual differences can play an important role in why some people are more prone to overthinking than others.

Genetic factors, cognitive styles, and personality traits can contribute to excessive thinking and rumination. While some of these factors may be innate, others can be influenced by environmental factors, personal experiences, and individual coping strategies. By understanding the role of individual differences in overthinking, individuals can work towards developing strategies to manage and reduce excessive thinking, improving their mental health and overall well-being.

Excessive thinking can be a complex and multifactorial behavior that can significantly impact mental health and overall quality of life. The physical nature of overthinking involves various brain regions, including the prefrontal cortex and amygdala. Triggers for excessive thinking can include stressful life events, mental health disorders, personality traits, and environmental factors. Individual differences, such as genetic predisposition and cognitive style, can also explain why some people are more prone to overthinking than others. By understanding the causes and triggers of overthinking, individuals can work towards developing strategies to manage and reduce excessive thinking, improving their mental health and overall well-being.

Support my Work

If you enjoyed the contents of this book and want to help me in a simple, accessible, and fast way, I warmly invite you to leave an honest review directly on the Amazon product page. That way, other people looking for vegetarian recipes and other vegetarian diet-related content will find my book and all my work. To do this, use the camera on your smartphone to scan the QR code or click on this link if you have the reader in the digital version.

Thank you, Rudolf.

Recognize useless Thoughts

Recognizing useless thoughts is essential to help individuals manage their mental health and well-being. Vain thoughts refer to unproductive, repetitive, or harmful ideas that do not serve any useful purpose. In this chapter, we will explore what learning to recognize useless thoughts means, including their benefits and how they can be achieved.

Useless thoughts can be a significant source of stress and anxiety for many people. When people engage in vain thoughts, they may be trapped in a cycle of rumination, negative thinking, and worry. These thoughts can be unproductive and do not lead to effective problem-solving or decision-making. Moreover, they can be emotionally exhausting and adversely affect mental health and well-being.

Learning to recognize useless thoughts is an essential first step in managing excessive thinking and reducing feelings of stress and anxiety. Identifying vain thoughts involves becoming more aware of one's thinking patterns and developing an understanding of what thoughts are helpful and what thoughts are not. Individuals can create a more mindful and balanced approach to thinking and decision-making by learning to recognize useless thoughts.

There are several strategies that individuals can use to learn to recognize useless thoughts. These include mindfulness meditation, cognitive-behavioral therapy, and journaling.

Mindfulness meditation involves focusing one's attention on the present moment without judgment or distraction. This can help individuals become more aware of their thinking patterns and develop a more mindful approach.

Journaling can also be an effective way of learning to recognize useless thoughts. By writing down one's thoughts and feelings, individuals can become more aware of their thinking patterns and better understand helpful ideas. This can be a valuable tool in creating a more mindful and balanced approach to thinking.

Recognizing useless thoughts can have several benefits for mental health and well-being. First, individuals can develop greater control over their thoughts and emotions by becoming more aware of their thinking patterns. This can lead to reduced feelings of stress and anxiety and increased feelings of calm and contentment.

Recognizing useless thoughts can also lead to more effective problem-solving and decision-making. By identifying unproductive or harmful thinking patterns, individuals can develop a more balanced and rational approach to decision-making, leading to more positive outcomes and reduced stress and anxiety.

What's Positive Thinking?

Positive thinking refers to a mental attitude or mindset that emphasizes the positive aspects of life and situations. Positive thinking involves focusing on one's strengths and opportunities rather than one's weaknesses and limitations. This chapter will explore positive thinking, its benefits, and how to cultivate a positive mindset.

Positive thinking is a mindset that involves focusing on positive thoughts and emotions and maintaining a positive outlook on life. Positive thinking can involve a variety of cognitive strategies, including reframing negative situations, visualizing success, and practicing gratitude.

Positive thinking involves the use of positive self-talk and language. This can include using affirmations or positive statements to reinforce positive beliefs and attitudes. Positive thinking can also involve reframing negative situations and thoughts by looking for positive aspects or opportunities.

Positive thinking has been associated with several benefits for mental and physical health. Some of these benefits include:

1. **Reduced stress and anxiety**: Positive thinking can help individuals manage stress and anxiety by promoting a sense of calm and positivity. Positive thinking can help individuals reframe negative situations, reducing the impact of stress and strain on mental and physical health.
2. **Improved mood and emotional well-being:** Positive thinking has been shown to improve mood and

emotional well-being, promoting feelings of happiness, contentment, and positivity.

3. **Improved relationships:** Positive thinking can improve relationships by promoting a more positive and empathetic attitude toward others. Positive thinking can also lead to more effective communication and problem-solving in relationships.

4. **Increased resilience:** Positive thinking can help individuals become more resilient in facing challenges and setbacks. Positive thinking can promote a sense of optimism and hope, even in difficult situations.

Cultivating a positive mindset involves developing habits and strategies that promote positive thinking and emotional well-being. Some strategies for cultivating a positive attitude include:

1. Practicing gratitude involves focusing on the positive aspects of one's life and expressing gratitude for these things. This can include keeping a gratitude journal or simply taking time each day to reflect on what one is grateful for.

2. **Using positive self-talk:** Positive self-talk involves using positive language and affirmations to reinforce positive beliefs and attitudes. This can include using positive statements like "I am capable" or "I am worthy" to promote a positive self-image.

3. **Visualizing success:** Visualizing success involves imagining positive outcomes and successes. This can help individuals build confidence and motivation and promote a positive attitude towards goal setting and achievement.

4. **Surrounding oneself with positive influences:** Positive people, media, and experiences can promote a positive outlook. This can involve spending time with supportive friends and family or engaging in activities that promote positivity and emotional well-being.

Positive thinking is a mindset that involves focusing on the positive aspects of life and situations and maintaining a positive outlook on life. Positive thinking has several benefits for mental and physical health, including reduced stress and anxiety, improved mood and emotional well-being, improved relationships, and increased resilience. Cultivating a positive mindset involves developing habits and strategies that promote positive thinking and emotional well-being, such as practicing gratitude, using positive self-talk, visualizing success, and surrounding oneself with positive influences. By cultivating a positive mindset, individuals can improve their mental and physical health and lead happier, more fulfilling lives.

What's Productive Thinking?

Productive thinking refers to a type of thinking that is focused on solving problems and achieving goals. On the other hand, constructive thinking involves using rational and analytical strategies to identify and evaluate possible solutions to a problem. This chapter will explore productive thinking, its benefits, and how to cultivate an abundant mindset.

Productive thinking is a type of thinking that is focused on solving problems and achieving goals. Constructive thinking involves several cognitive strategies, including:

- **Analyzing the problem:** Productive thinking involves analyzing the problem or situation to identify its key features and underlying causes.
- **Generating alternatives:** Productive thinking involves developing multiple options or solutions to the problem or situation.

- **Evaluating alternatives:** Productive thinking involves assessing the strengths and weaknesses of each option to determine the best course of action.
- **Implementing solutions:** Productive thinking involves implementing the chosen solution and monitoring its effectiveness.

Productive thinking has been associated with several benefits for personal and professional success. Some of these benefits include:

- **Improved problem-solving skills:** Productive thinking can help individuals develop better problem-solving skills by promoting a more analytical and rational approach to problem-solving.
- **Improved decision-making skills:** Productive thinking can also help individuals develop better decision-making skills by promoting a more rational and systematic approach to decision-making.
- **Increased creativity:** Productive thinking can help individuals become more creative by promoting the generation of multiple alternatives and solutions to a problem or situation.
- **Improved productivity:** Productive thinking can help individuals become more productive by

promoting a more efficient and practical approach to problem-solving and decision-making.

Cultivating a productive mindset involves developing habits and strategies that promote constructive thinking and problem-solving. Some methods for producing a practical attitude include:

Developing a growth mindset: Developing a growth mindset involves adopting a positive attitude towards learning and growth. This can include viewing challenges and setbacks as opportunities for learning and improvement and seeking feedback and constructive criticism to improve one's skills and abilities.

Setting goals can help individuals focus their thinking and efforts toward achieving specific outcomes. Plans can be used to prioritize tasks and activities and to provide a sense of direction and purpose.

Managing time effectively: Managing time effectively involves prioritizing tasks and activities and using time management strategies to maximize productivity and efficiency.

Seeking feedback and collaboration: Seeking feedback and partnership can help individuals identify areas for improvement and generate new ideas and solutions to problems.

P thinking is a type of thinking that is focused on solving problems and achieving goals. Productive thinking involves several cognitive strategies, including analyzing the situation, generating alternatives, evaluating alternatives, and implementing solutions. Constructive thinking has several benefits for personal and professional success, including improved problem-solving, decision-making, creativity, and productivity. Cultivating a productive mindset involves developing habits and strategies that promote constructive thinking and problem-solving, such as creating a growth mindset, setting goals, managing time effectively, and seeking feedback and collaboration. By cultivating a productive mindset, individuals can improve their problem-solving and decision-making skills, increase their creativity, and achieve tremendous success in their personal and professional lives.

What Is Persistent Thinking?

Persistent thinking refers to a pattern of repetitive or intrusive thoughts that can be difficult to control or manage. Constant thinking can involve a variety of harmful or distressing thoughts, including worries, fears, or obsessions. This chapter will explore persistent review, its causes, and how to manage it.

Persistent thinking refers to a pattern of repetitive or intrusive thoughts that can be difficult to control or manage. Constant review can be characterized by negative or distressing thoughts, including worries, fears, or obsessions. Persistent thinking can disrupt daily life, interfering with one's ability to focus, sleep, or engage in everyday activities.

Persistent thinking can be caused by various factors, including stress, anxiety, trauma, or mental health conditions. Constant thinking can also be a symptom of diseases such as obsessive-compulsive disorder (OCD) or post-traumatic stress disorder (PTSD).

The symptoms of persistent thinking can vary depending on the individual and the underlying cause of the constant review. However, four common symptoms of persistent thought include:

1. **Repetitive or intrusive thoughts:** Persistent thinking can involve repetitive or intrusive thoughts that can be difficult to control or manage.
2. **Difficulty concentrating:** Persistent thinking can interfere with one's ability to concentrate or focus on daily tasks or activities.
3. **Sleep disturbances:** Persistent thinking can cause sleep disturbances, including difficulty falling or staying asleep or nightmares.
4. **Physical symptoms:** Persistent thinking can also cause physical symptoms such as headaches, muscle tension, or fatigue.

Persistent thinking can be caused by various factors, including stress, anxiety, trauma, or mental health conditions. Constant thinking can also be a symptom of diseases such as obsessive-compulsive disorder (OCD) or post-traumatic stress disorder (PTSD).

- **Stress and Anxiety:** Stress and anxiety can contribute to persistent thinking by increasing the activation of the body's stress response, leading to increased rumination and negative thinking.
- **Trauma:** Trauma can also contribute to persistent thinking, as individuals may experience intrusive thoughts related to the traumatic event.
- **Mental Health Conditions:** Mental health conditions such as OCD or PTSD can cause persistent thinking as a symptom of the disease.

Managing persistent thinking involves developing strategies and habits to help individuals manage their thoughts and emotions more effectively. Some strategies for managing constant review include:

- Mindfulness meditation involves focusing on the present moment without judgment or distraction. Mindfulness meditation can reduce persistent thinking by helping individuals develop a more mindful and accepting attitude toward their thoughts and emotions.
- **Exercise:** Exercise can effectively reduce stress and anxiety, which can contribute to persistent thinking. Regular exercise can help regulate cortisol levels and

promote the production of endorphins, improving mood and reducing feelings of stress and anxiety.

- **Relaxation techniques:** Relaxation techniques such as deep breathing, progressive muscle relaxation, or visualization can reduce persistent thinking and promote peace and calm.

Persistent thinking refers to a pattern of repetitive or intrusive thoughts that can be difficult to control or manage. Constant review can be caused by various factors, including stress, anxiety, trauma, or mental health conditions. Managing consistent thinking involves developing strategies and habits to help individuals manage their thoughts and emotions more effectively. Techniques such as mindfulness meditation, cognitive behavior

How to stop dwelling on negative thoughts

Dwelling negative thoughts can be a common and challenging experience for many people. Negative thoughts can be persistent and difficult to shake, leading to feelings of anxiety, depression, and low self-esteem. However, some strategies can be used to stop dwelling on negative thoughts and promote a more positive mindset.

- *Acknowledge and accept negative thoughts:* The first step in stopping them is acknowledging and taking them. It's essential to recognize that negative thoughts are a normal part of life, and everyone experiences them at some point. Avoiding or suppressing negative thoughts makes them more persistent, so it's essential to acknowledge and accept them without judgment.
- *Challenge negative thoughts:* Challenging them is essential once negative thoughts are acknowledged and accepted. Negative reviews are often based on distorted or inaccurate thinking patterns, so it can be helpful to question and challenge the validity of these thoughts. Ask yourself if there is evidence to

support the negative review or if there are alternative explanations for the situation.

- *Practice gratitude:* Practicing gratitude can be an effective way of reducing negative thinking patterns. By focusing on the positive aspects of life, individuals can shift their attention away from negative thoughts and emotions. This can involve keeping a gratitude journal or simply taking time each day to reflect on what one is grateful for.
- *Engage in positive self-talk:* Positive self-talk can help individuals counteract negative thoughts and promote a more positive mindset. This can involve using positive statements like "I am capable" or "I am worthy" to reinforce positive beliefs and attitudes.
- *Practice mindfulness:* Mindfulness meditation involves focusing on the present moment without judgment or distraction. By practicing mindfulness, individuals can become more aware of their negative thoughts and emotions and develop a more mindful and accepting attitude toward them.
- *Engage in physical activity:* Physical activity can effectively reduce negative thoughts and promote a more positive mindset. Exercise can help regulate

- cortisol levels and stimulate the production of endorphins, improving mood and reducing feelings of stress and anxiety.
- *Seek support:* Talking to friends, family, or a mental health professional can effectively reduce negative thoughts and promote a more positive mindset. Talking to others can help individuals gain perspective on their thoughts and emotions and develop more effective coping strategies.

Dwelling on negative thoughts can be a challenging experience. Still, some strategies can be used to stop negative thoughts and promote a more positive mindset. Procedures such as acknowledging and accepting negative thoughts, challenging negative thoughts, practicing gratitude, engaging in positive self-talk, practicing mindfulness, engaging in physical activity, and seeking support can all effectively reduce negative thoughts and promote a more positive mindset. By incorporating these strategies into daily life, individuals can improve their mental and emotional well-being and lead happier, more fulfilling lives.

Practical Strategies for Managing Persistent Thinking

Persistent thinking can be a challenging experience, and it can interfere with daily life by causing negative emotions, distracting from work or activities, and interfering with sleep. However, practical strategies can be used to manage persistent thinking and promote a more positive mindset. This chapter will explore practical strategies for managing constant thinking, including mindfulness meditation, cognitive-behavioral therapy, and lifestyle changes.

Mindfulness Meditation:

Mindfulness meditation is a type of meditation that involves focusing one's attention on the present moment without judgment or distraction. Mindfulness meditation is an effective strategy for managing persistent thinking by promoting a more mindful and accepting attitude toward one's thoughts and emotions.

One practical strategy for incorporating mindfulness meditation into daily life is to set aside a specific time each day for meditation practice. This can involve sitting in a quiet, comfortable space, focusing on one's breath, and allowing thoughts and emotions to come and go without judgment or distraction. Over time, regular mindfulness meditation practice can help individuals become more aware of their thoughts and feelings and develop a more mindful and accepting attitude toward them.

Cognitive-Behavioral Therapy:

Cognitive-behavioral therapy (CBT) is a type of therapy that focuses on changing negative thought patterns and behaviors. CBT can be an effective strategy for managing persistent thinking by helping individuals identify and challenge negative thoughts and develop more effective coping strategies.

One practical strategy for incorporating CBT into daily life is working with a mental health professional specializing in CBT. During therapy sessions, individuals can learn specific techniques for identifying and challenging negative thoughts, such as cognitive restructuring or behavioral experiments. Individuals can also work with their therapist to develop a personalized treatment plan incorporating specific strategies for managing persistent thinking.

Lifestyle Changes:

Lifestyle changes can also be an effective strategy for managing persistent thinking. This can involve changing one's diet, exercise routine, or sleep habits to promote overall health and well-being.

One practical strategy for incorporating lifestyle changes into daily life is to start small and make gradual changes over time. For example, individuals can begin by incorporating more fruits and vegetables into their diet or adding a 10-minute walk to their daily routine. Over time, individuals can gradually increase the intensity and duration of their exercise routine or make more significant changes to their diet or sleep habits.

Persistent thinking can be a challenging experience, but there are practical strategies that can be used to manage constant thinking and promote a more positive mindset. Techniques such as mindfulness meditation, cognitive-behavioral therapy, and lifestyle changes can reduce persistent thinking and promote mental and emotional well-being. By incorporating these strategies into daily life, individuals can develop more effective coping strategies, improve their mental and emotional health, and lead happier, more fulfilling lives.

Management of anxiety and panic

Anxiety and panic can be challenging experiences that can interfere with daily life by causing distressing physical symptoms, limiting activities, and contributing to negative emotions. However, practical strategies can be used to manage anxiety and panic and promote a more positive mindset. This chapter will explore practical strategies for managing anxiety and panic that do not involve cognitive-behavioral therapy, relaxation techniques, or lifestyle changes.

Physical Activity:
Physical activity can effectively manage anxiety and panic by reducing stress levels and promoting the release of endorphins,

natural mood boosters. In addition to these benefits, regular physical activity can improve overall physical health and reduce the risk of chronic diseases such as heart disease and diabetes.

There are various options when it comes to incorporating physical activity into daily life. One practical strategy is to find an activity that is enjoyable and sustainable. This can involve walking, jogging, cycling, swimming, or yoga. Engaging in physical activity with a friend or family member can also be a helpful way to stay motivated and accountable.

Another practical strategy is to set achievable goals and track progress over time. This can involve developing a plan to walk for 30 minutes daily or attending a yoga class once a week. Tracking progress can help individuals see the positive impact of physical activity on their mental and physical well-being and can help reinforce the habit of regular physical activity.

Finally, it's important to remember that physical activity does not have to be intense or time-consuming to be effective. Even small amounts of physical activity can positively impact mental and physical health. In fact, research has shown that just 10 minutes of moderate physical activity can improve mood and reduce anxiety levels.

Physical activity is an essential strategy for managing anxiety and panic by promoting the release of endorphins and reducing stress levels. By finding an enjoyable and sustainable activity, setting achievable goals, tracking progress, and remembering that even small amounts of physical activity can be adequate, individuals can improve their mental and physical well-being and lead happier, more fulfilling lives.

Self-Care:

Self-care is essential for managing anxiety and panic by promoting mental and emotional well-being. Self-care can involve various activities that promote relaxation, enjoyment, and positive self-esteem.

One practical strategy for incorporating self-care into daily life is to set aside time each day for an activity that promotes relaxation or enjoyment. This can involve activities such as reading, taking a bath, listening to music, or spending time with loved ones. Self-care activities can help individuals reduce stress and improve mental and emotional well-being.

Managing anxiety and panic can be a challenging experience. Still, practical strategies can be used to address these conditions and promote a more positive mindset. Techniques such as mindfulness, physical activity, and self-care can all be effective in reducing anxiety and panic symptoms and promoting mental and emotional well-being. By incorporating these strategies into daily life, individuals can develop more effective coping strategies, improve their mental and emotional health, and lead happier, more fulfilling lives.

Meditation

Meditation is a practice that has been used for centuries to promote mental and emotional well-being. Meditation involves focusing on the present moment without judgment or distraction. Meditation can be a helpful tool for managing anxiety and stress and promoting a more positive mindset. This chapter will explore practical strategies for incorporating meditation into daily life, including mindfulness, mantra meditation, and loving-kindness meditation.

Mindfulness Meditation:

Mindfulness meditation is a type of meditation that involves focusing one's attention on the present moment without judgment or distraction. Mindfulness meditation can effectively manage anxiety and stress by promoting awareness of one's thoughts and emotions and reducing negative thinking patterns.

One practical strategy for incorporating mindfulness meditation into daily life is to set aside a few minutes daily to practice mindfulness meditation. This can involve sitting in a quiet, comfortable space, focusing on one's breath, and allowing thoughts and emotions to come and go without judgment or distraction. Over time, regular mindfulness meditation practice can help individuals become more aware of their thoughts and feelings and develop a more mindful and accepting attitude toward them.

Mantra Meditation:

Mantra meditation is a type of meditation that involves repeating a phrase or word to focus the mind and promote relaxation. The term "mantra" comes from the Sanskrit language and can be translated to mean "mind tool" or "mind instrument."

One of the critical benefits of mantra meditation is that it provides a positive focus for the mind, helping to reduce negative thinking patterns and promote relaxation. Mantras can be chosen based on personal significance or meaning and repeated silently to oneself during meditation practice.

When it comes to incorporating mantra meditation into daily life, a few practical strategies can be helpful. One method is to choose a mantra that has personal significance or meaning. This can involve selecting a word or phrase that represents a unique value or goal, such as "peace," "love," or "strength."

Another strategy is to establish a regular meditation practice that incorporates mantra meditation. This can involve setting aside a specific time each day to practice meditation, such as in the morning before starting the day or in the evening before going to bed. Individuals can incorporate mantra meditation into their daily routines by establishing a regular meditation practice.

Finally, it's important to remember that mantra meditation can be simple and inexpensive to be effective. However, even just a few minutes of mantra meditation practice each day can positively impact mental and emotional well-being. Over time, regular mantra meditation practice can help individuals promote relaxation, reduce stress levels, and develop a more positive mindset.

Mantra meditation is a powerful tool for managing anxiety and stress and promoting mental and emotional well-being. By choosing a mantra that has personal significance or meaning, establishing a regular meditation practice, and remembering that even a few minutes of exercise each day can be effective, individuals can develop the habit of incorporating mantra meditation into their daily routine and improve their overall mental and emotional health.

Loving-Kindness Meditation:

Loving-kindness meditation is a type of meditation that involves focusing on feelings of love and compassion towards oneself and others. It is also known as Metta meditation, with "Metta" being the Pali word for "loving-kindness" or "friendliness." This type of meditation is rooted in the Buddhist tradition. Still, it can be practiced by individuals of all backgrounds and beliefs.

One of the critical benefits of loving-kindness meditation is that it promotes positive emotions and reduces negative thinking patterns. By focusing on feelings of love and compassion towards oneself and others, individuals can cultivate a more positive mindset and develop greater empathy and understanding towards others.

When it comes to incorporating loving-kindness meditation into daily life, a few practical strategies can be helpful. One method is to set aside a specific time each day to practice loving-kindness meditation, such as in the morning before starting the day or in the evening before bed. During meditation, individuals can repeat phrases that promote love and compassion towards themselves and others.

These phrases can be tailored to personal preference but may include words such as:

- *May I be happy and at peace? May I be free from suffering?*
- *May I be filled with love and compassion?*
- *May all beings be comfortable and at ease.*
- *May all beings be free from suffering.*
- *May all beings be filled with love and compassion.*

Another practical strategy for incorporating loving-kindness meditation into daily life is to use visualizations or imagery to enhance the practice. This can involve visualizing oneself surrounded by love and compassion or imagining sending feelings of love and compassion to others.

Finally, it's important to remember that loving-kindness meditation can be a gradual process that requires patience and practice. However, regular loving-kindness meditation can help individuals develop greater empathy and understanding towards others, promote positive emotions, and reduce negative thinking patterns over time.

In conclusion, loving-kindness meditation is a powerful tool for managing anxiety and stress and promoting mental and emotional well-being. By setting aside a specific time each day to practice loving-kindness meditation, using visualizations or imagery to enhance the practice, and remembering that it is a gradual process that requires patience and practice, individuals can develop the habit of incorporating loving-kindness meditation into their daily routine and improve their overall mental and emotional health.

Meditation is a powerful tool for managing anxiety and stress and promoting mental and emotional well-being. Strategies such as mindfulness meditation, mantra meditation, and loving-kindness meditation can effectively reduce anxiety and promote a more positive mindset. By incorporating these strategies into daily life, individuals can develop more effective coping strategies, improve their mental and emotional health, and lead happier, more fulfilling lives.

Support my Work

If you enjoyed the contents of this book and want to help me in a simple, accessible, and fast way, I warmly invite you to leave an honest review directly on the Amazon product page. That way, other people looking for vegetarian recipes and other vegetarian diet-related content will find my book and all my work. To do this, use the camera on your smartphone to scan the QR code or click on this link if you have the reader in the digital version.

Thank you, Rudolf.

Gratitude and appreciation

Gratitude and appreciation are essential concepts that can significantly impact mental and emotional well-being. Gratitude involves recognizing and being thankful for the positive aspects of one's life. In contrast, appreciation involves recognizing the value and worth of oneself and others. In this chapter, we will explore the meaning and benefits of gratitude and appreciation and practical strategies for incorporating these concepts into daily life.

Gratitude:

Gratitude is recognizing and being thankful for the positive aspects of one's life. This can involve identifying the blessings in one's life, such as good health, supportive relationships, and meaningful work. Gratitude can also include recognizing the positive aspects of difficult or challenging situations, such as opportunities for growth or learning.

Practicing gratitude can have a significant impact on mental and emotional well-being. Research has shown that regularly practicing gratitude can improve mood, reduce stress, and increase happiness and contentment. Gratitude can also promote greater social connection, as individuals expressing gratitude are often perceived as likable and trustworthy.

A few practical strategies can help incorporate gratitude into daily life. One method is to keep a gratitude journal, in which individuals write down three to five things they are thankful for daily. Another strategy is to practice expressing gratitude directly to others through thank-you notes or verbal expressions of appreciation. Finally, it can be helpful to practice reframing negative situations in a positive light by recognizing opportunities for growth or learning.

Appreciation:

Appreciation involves recognizing the value and worth of oneself and others. This can include recognizing the positive qualities and contributions of oneself and others and expressing gratitude for their presence and impact on one's life.

Practicing appreciation can have a significant impact on mental and emotional well-being. Research has shown that regularly practicing gratitude improves self-esteem, reduces loneliness, and promotes greater social connection. Appreciation can also promote greater empathy and understanding toward others. Individuals who practice appreciation are often perceived as more compassionate and caring.

A few practical strategies can help incorporate appreciation into daily life. One method is to regularly practice recognizing and acknowledging the positive qualities and contributions of oneself and others. This can involve expressing gratitude directly to others or practicing self-appreciation through positive affirmations or self-talk. Another strategy is to practice mindfulness, which can help individuals become more aware of the positive aspects of their life and the contributions of others.

Gratitude and appreciation are essential concepts that can significantly impact mental and emotional well-being. Regularly practicing gratitude and appreciation can improve their mood, reduce stress levels, promote social connection, and develop empathy and understanding toward others. Practical strategies for incorporating gratitude and appreciation into daily life include keeping a gratitude journal, expressing gratitude directly to others, practicing mindfulness, and practicing self-appreciation. By combining these strategies into everyday life, individuals can improve their mental and emotional health and lead happier, more fulfilling lives.

How To Reduce Stress

Stress is a normal and often unavoidable part of life. However, when stress levels become too high or chronic, they can significantly negatively impact mental and physical health. In this chapter, we will explore why it is essential to reduce stress, the adverse effects that stress can cause, the main benefits of stress reduction, and practical techniques for reducing stress.

Why It is Important to Reduce Stress:

Reducing stress is essential because chronic stress can significantly negatively impact mental and physical health. Chronic stress can lead to various health problems, including high blood pressure, heart disease, anxiety, depression, and sleep problems. By reducing stress, individuals can promote better overall health and well-being.

Adverse Effects of Stress:

Stress can have a range of adverse effects on mental and physical health. These effects can be short-term or long-term and can vary in severity depending on the individual and the stress level experienced. Here are some of the most common adverse effects of stress:

- **Increased Risk of Heart Disease and Stroke:** Chronic stress can increase the risk of heart disease and stroke by raising blood pressure, improving cholesterol levels, and promoting plaque buildup in the arteries. This can lead to cardiovascular problems, including heart attack, stroke, and angina.
- **Weakened Immune System:** Chronic stress can weaken the immune system, making individuals more susceptible to illness and infection. This is because stress hormones, such as cortisol, can

suppress immune system function and make it more difficult for the body to fight harmful pathogens.

- **Increased Risk of Anxiety and Depression:** Chronic stress can increase the risk of anxiety and depression by promoting the release of stress hormones and causing changes in brain chemistry. This can lead to feelings of sadness, hopelessness, despair, and a range of physical symptoms such as fatigue, insomnia, and appetite changes.
- **Insomnia or Other Sleep Problems:** Chronic stress can cause insomnia or other sleep problems by disrupting the body's natural sleep-wake cycle. This can lead to feelings of exhaustion, irritability, and difficulty concentrating during the day.
- **Digestive Problems:** Chronic stress can cause digestive problems, such as irritable bowel syndrome (IBS), by promoting inflammation in the digestive tract and disrupting the balance of beneficial bacteria in the gut. This can lead to symptoms such as abdominal pain, bloating, and changes in bowel habits.
- **Chronic Pain or Tension Headaches:** Chronic stress can cause chronic pain or tension headaches by

promoting muscle tension and increasing inflammation in the body. This can lead to feelings of discomfort, fatigue, and difficulty concentrating.

In addition to these physical effects, chronic stress can adversely affect mental health and quality of life. For example, chronic stress can lead to feelings of overwhelm, burnout, and disconnection from others. It can also make it more difficult for individuals to engage in healthy behaviors, such as exercise, healthy eating, and getting enough sleep. Therefore, reducing stress is essential for promoting better mental and physical health and improving the overall quality of life.

Benefits of Stress Reduction:

Reducing stress can have a range of benefits for mental and physical health. These benefits can be short-term or long-term and can vary in severity depending on the individual and the stress level experienced. Here are some of the most common uses of stress reduction:

- **Improved Overall Health and Well-being:** Reducing stress can promote overall health and well-being by reducing the adverse effects of stress on the body and mind. This can lead to improved physical health, such as reduced blood pressure, improved immune system function, and reduced inflammation. It can also improve mental health, such as reduced anxiety and depression symptoms, improved mood, and increased happiness and contentment.

- **Reduced Risk of Heart Disease and Stroke:** Reducing stress can lower the risk of heart disease and stroke by promoting better cardiovascular health. This can be achieved through various stress-reducing techniques, such as exercise, meditation, and deep breathing.
- **Improved Immune System Function:** Reducing stress can improve immune system function by reducing the adverse effects of stress hormones on the body. This can lead to a more robust immune system, better protecting the body from illness and infection.
- **Reduced Anxiety and Depression Symptoms:** Reducing stress can reduce symptoms of anxiety and depression by promoting a more positive outlook and reducing negative thinking patterns. This can lead to improved mental health outcomes and better quality of life.

- **Improved Sleep Quality and Duration:** Reducing stress can enhance sleep quality and duration by promoting relaxation and reducing muscle tension. This can lead to improved energy levels, better cognitive function, and improved mood.
- **Reduced Pain and Tension Headaches:** Reducing stress can reduce chronic pain and tension headaches by promoting relaxation and reducing muscle tension. This can improve quality of life and overall physical and mental health.

Overall, reducing stress can have a significant positive impact on mental and physical health and improve the overall quality of life. By incorporating stress-reducing techniques into daily life, individuals can improve their health and well-being and lead happier, more fulfilling lives.

Reducing stress is essential for promoting overall health and well-being. Chronic stress can have various adverse effects on mental and physical health. Reducing stress can promote better health outcomes and improve quality of life. Techniques for reducing stress include exercise, mindfulness meditation, deep breathing, time management, and social support. By incorporating these techniques into daily life, individuals can reduce stress levels, promote better mental and physical health, and lead happier, more fulfilling lives.

How To Reduce Overthinking

Overthinking is a common problem that can lead to anxiety, stress, and other adverse mental health outcomes. Overthinking involves spending excessive time and energy analyzing and dwelling on past events or future possibilities, often leading to a sense of paralysis and inability to make decisions. This chapter will explore practical strategies for reducing overthinking and promoting better mental health.

Why is it Important to Reduce Overthinking:

Reducing overthinking is essential for several reasons related to mental health and well-being. Here are some additional details about why it is critical to lowering overthinking:

- Reduced Anxiety and Stress Levels: Overthinking can increase anxiety and stress levels by promoting negative thinking patterns and worrying about future events. By reducing overthinking, individuals can lower their anxiety and stress levels, improving their mental and physical health.
- **Improved Decision-Making Ability:** Overthinking can interfere with decision-making, causing paralysis and indecisiveness. By reducing

overthinking, individuals can enhance their ability to make decisions and act in their lives.

- **Increased Productivity and Creativity:** Overthinking can drain productivity and creativity by taking up mental space and causing distraction. Individuals can free up mental space and promote better productivity and creativity by reducing overthinking.
- **Improved Relationships with Others:** Overthinking can interfere with relationships by causing individuals to overanalyze social situations and become overly self-conscious. By reducing overthinking, individuals can improve their relationships with others and feel more comfortable in social situations.
- **Increased Sense of Peace and Contentment:** Overthinking can lead to feelings of overwhelm and dissatisfaction with life. Individuals can promote a greater sense of peace and contentment by reducing overthinking.

Reducing overthinking is essential for promoting better mental and physical health, improving decision-making ability, increasing productivity and creativity, improving relationships, and promoting a greater sense of peace and contentment. Individuals can improve their overall quality of life and well-being by recognizing the importance of reducing overthinking and incorporating strategies into daily life.

Reducing overthinking can have a range of benefits for mental and physical health. Here are 5 additional details about the benefits of lowering overthinking:

1. **Reduced Anxiety and Stress Levels:** Overthinking can increase anxiety and stress levels by promoting negative thinking patterns and worrying about future events. By reducing overthinking, individuals can lower their anxiety and stress levels, improving their mental and physical health. They can feel more relaxed and at ease in their daily lives.

2. **Improved Decision-Making Ability:** Overthinking can interfere with decision-making, causing paralysis and indecisiveness. By reducing overthinking, individuals can enhance their ability to make decisions and act in their lives. They can make more confident decisions based on their gut instincts.

3. **Increased Productivity and Creativity:** Overthinking can drain productivity and creativity by taking up mental space and causing

distraction. Individuals can free up mental space and promote better productivity and creativity by reducing overthinking. They can work more efficiently and think more creatively.

4. **Improved Relationships with Others:** Overthinking can interfere with relationships by causing individuals to overanalyze social situations and become overly self-conscious. By reducing overthinking, individuals can improve their relationships with others and feel more comfortable in social situations. They can connect with others more authentically.

5. **Increased Sense of Peace and Contentment:** Overthinking can lead to feelings of overwhelm and dissatisfaction with life. Individuals can promote a greater sense of peace and contentment by reducing overthinking. They can focus on the present moment and appreciate the small joys in life.

Reducing overthinking is essential for promoting better mental and physical health, improving decision-making ability, increasing productivity and creativity, improving relationships, and promoting a greater sense of peace and contentment. By practicing techniques for reducing overthinking and incorporating them into daily life, individuals can enjoy these benefits and lead happier, more fulfilling lives.

In conclusion, reducing overthinking is essential for promoting better mental health and well-being. Overthinking can lead to increased stress and anxiety, interfere with decision-making and lead to a sense of paralysis. Techniques for reducing overthinking include mindfulness meditation, cognitive behavioral therapy, journaling, exercise, and limiting social media and news consumption. By incorporating these techniques into daily life, individuals can reduce overthinking, improve mental and physical health, and lead happier, more fulfilling lives.

Improve Sleep

Many struggles with getting adequate sleep, which can lead to many negative consequences for physical and mental health. Improving sleep habits is a critical component of maintaining overall well-being. Still, it can be challenging to know where to start. In this discussion, we will explore some effective strategies for improving sleep.

Establish a consistent sleep schedule: Try to go to bed and wake up simultaneously every day, even on weekends. This can help regulate your body's internal clock, making it easier to fall asleep and wake up naturally.

Create a relaxing sleep environment: Keep your bedroom calm, dark, and quiet. Consider investing in blackout curtains or earplugs if necessary. Use comfortable bedding and pillows that suit your preferences.

Practice good sleep hygiene: Avoid caffeine, alcohol, and electronic devices for several hours before bedtime. Develop a relaxing bedtime routine, such as taking a warm bath or reading a book.

Exercise regularly: Regular physical activity can help promote better sleep. Aim for at least 30 minutes of moderate intensity exercise most days of the week.

Manage stress: Stress can interfere with sleep quality. Practice relaxation techniques, such as deep breathing or meditation, to reduce stress and promote relaxation.

Try aromatherapy: Certain scents like lavender or chamomile can promote relaxation and improve sleep quality. Also, try using essential oils or a diffuser in your bedroom.

Use a white noise machine: White noise machines can help block out external noise and create a calming environment for sleep.

Try a weighted blanket: Weighted blankets can provide comfort and security, promoting relaxation and improving sleep quality.

Improving sleep habits can have a significant impact on overall health and well-being. By establishing a consistent sleep schedule, creating a relaxing sleep environment, practicing good sleep hygiene, exercising regularly, and managing stress, you can improve sleep quality and feel more rested and refreshed. Additionally, trying out stimulating proposals like aromatherapy, using a white noise machine, or using a weighted blanket can help promote better sleep. Experimenting with different strategies and finding what works best for you is essential.

Sleep Hygiene

A regular sleep schedule is essential because it helps regulate the body's internal clock. Going to bed and waking up at the same time every day, even on weekends, can promote better quality sleep.

Creating a relaxing sleep environment can involve several strategies, such as using comfortable bedding, maintaining a calm and quiet sleeping space, and reducing exposure to light and noise. It can also include minimizing electronic devices before bedtime, as the blue light emitted by these devices can interfere with the body's natural sleep-wake cycle.

Avoiding stimulating activities before bedtime can also help promote better sleep. This can include exercising, eating heavy meals, and consuming caffeine or alcohol in the hours leading up to rest.

Engaging in relaxing activities before bedtime can help promote better sleep. This can include taking a warm bath, reading a book, or practicing relaxation techniques like deep breathing or meditation.

Maintaining a consistent sleep schedule, even on weekends, can be challenging for some people. Still, it can help promote better sleep. If you need to adjust your sleep schedule occasionally, try to do so gradually over a few days rather than all at once.

Good sleep hygiene can help promote restful and restorative sleep and improve overall health and well-being. By incorporating these strategies into your daily routine, you can improve the quality of your sleep and feel more rested and refreshed each day.

Relaxation Techniques for Sleep

Relaxation techniques can help promote better sleep by calming the mind and body. One effective technique is deep breathing, where you take slow, deep breaths through your nose and out through your mouth, focusing on your breath and letting go of distracting thoughts.

Another technique is progressive muscle relaxation, where you tense and relax different muscle groups in the body, starting at your toes and moving up to your head.

Visualization is also helpful for promoting relaxation. First, close your eyes and imagine a calming and peaceful environment like a beach or forest. Then, engage all your senses in the visualization to fully immerse yourself in the background.

Mindfulness meditation is another technique for promoting relaxation. Sit quietly and focus on your breath, observing your thoughts and feelings without judgment.

Incorporating yoga into your daily routine is also helpful for reducing stress and promoting relaxation. Yoga combines physical postures with deep breathing and mindfulness to promote peace and reduce tension in the body.

Practicing these relaxation techniques regularly can promote better sleep and improve your overall health and well-being. Incorporating these techniques into your daily routine can help you feel more relaxed and refreshed and promote better quality sleep.

Addressing Sleep Disorders

Addressing sleep disorders is essential for promoting better sleep and overall health. Sleep disorders can have many underlying causes, such as medical conditions, medication side effects, or lifestyle factors. It's essential to identify the root cause of your sleep disorder to develop an effective treatment plan. Talk to your healthcare provider about your symptoms and any potential underlying causes.

Improving sleep hygiene can be an effective way to address sleep disorders. This involves creating a relaxing sleep environment, practicing relaxation techniques, and establishing a regular sleep schedule. In addition, avoiding caffeine, alcohol, and electronic devices before bedtime can improve sleep hygiene.

In some cases, medications may be necessary to treat sleep disorders. For example, your healthcare provider may prescribe sleep aids or other drugs to help you fall asleep and stay asleep. However, it's important to use medications as directed and only under the guidance of your healthcare provider.

Alternative therapies such as acupuncture or massage therapy can help promote relaxation and reduce stress, improving sleep quality.

Addressing sleep disorders can promote better sleep and improve your overall health and well-being. Incorporating these strategies into your daily routine can help you feel more rested and refreshed and promote better quality sleep.

How to reduce Nighttime thinking

Nighttime thinking, or ruminating thoughts that keep you awake at night, can be a frustrating and exhausting experience. Not only can it interfere with your ability to fall asleep, but it can also negatively impact your overall well-being. This discussion will explore some effective strategies for reducing Nighttime thinking.

Reducing Nighttime thinking is essential to promote better sleep and overall well-being. Unfortunately, many people experience Nighttime thinking, making it challenging to fall asleep and stay asleep. Here are some effective strategies to reduce Nighttime reflection:

Practice relaxation techniques: Engage in activities that promote relaxation, such as deep breathing, progressive muscle relaxation, or visualization. These techniques can help calm the mind and body, making it easier to fall asleep. Relaxation techniques can be done before bedtime or if you wake up at night and struggle to fall back asleep.

Develop a relaxing bedtime routine: Establishing a consistent bedtime routine can help reduce Nighttime thinking. This can include activities that promote relaxation, such as reading a book, taking a warm bath, or practicing yoga. The goal is to signal your body that it's time to wind down and prepare for sleep.

Limit exposure to stimulating activities: Avoid engaging in stimulating activities, such as using electronic devices or watching TV, for several hours before bedtime. These activities can interfere with sleep and exacerbate Nighttime thinking. Instead, engage in calming activities like reading or listening to soft music.

Write down your thoughts and worries: Keeping a journal to write down any reviews or concerns before bedtime can help release them from your mind and prevent rumination. Writing down your thoughts can help you process and reflect on them, making it easier to let them go and drift off to sleep.

Seek professional help: If Nighttime thinking persists despite your best efforts, consider seeking help from a mental health professional. They can help you identify underlying issues and develop an effective treatment plan. Sometimes, nighttime thinking can be a symptom of an underlying mental health condition, such as anxiety or depression. In these cases, professional help can be invaluable in managing these conditions and reducing Nighttime thinking.

In addition to these strategies, you can make other lifestyle changes to promote better sleep and reduce Nighttime thinking. Eating a balanced diet, engaging in regular physical activity, and managing stress are essential to improving sleep quality. By reducing Nighttime reflection, you can improve your ability to fall asleep and stay asleep, allowing you to wake up feeling refreshed and energized.

Reducing Nighttime thinking can be a challenging process. Still, you can improve your ability to fall and stay asleep by practicing relaxation techniques, establishing a consistent bedtime routine, limiting exposure to stimulating activities, keeping a journal, and seeking professional help. Experimenting with different strategies and finding what works best for you is essential. Reducing Nighttime thinking can promote better sleep and improve overall health and well-being.

Support my Work

If you enjoyed the contents of this book and want to help me in a simple, accessible, and fast way, I warmly invite you to leave an honest review directly on the Amazon product page. That way, other people looking for vegetarian recipes and other vegetarian diet-related content will find my book and all my work. To do this, use the camera on your smartphone to scan the QR code or click on this link if you have the reader in the digital version.

Thank you, Rudolf.

Time Management

Managing personal time is a vital skill that can lead to greater productivity, success, and overall well-being. However, in today's fast-paced world, balancing work, family life, and other commitments can be challenging. This is where effective time management comes into play. Time management is organizing and planning how to allocate time effectively, prioritizing tasks, and achieving goals promptly.

Effective time management can help individuals reduce stress, achieve their goals, and maximize their available time. It involves setting clear priorities, planning, and organizing tasks, and making intelligent decisions about how to use one's time. By managing time effectively, individuals can stay focused, avoid distractions, and increase productivity.

Poor time management, on the other hand, can lead to stress, burnout, and missed deadlines. In addition, it can result in a lack of productivity, missed opportunities, and decreased work-life balance. Therefore, individuals need to learn effective time management strategies to help them stay on top of their goals and commitments.

Managing personal time is crucial for success and overall well-being. Effective time management involves prioritizing tasks, organizing, and planning, and making intelligent decisions about how to use one's time. It can lead to greater productivity, reduced stress, and a more fulfilling life.

There are 7 strategies that individuals can use to better manage their time. Here are some of the main strategies:

1. **Create a schedule:** A plan can help individuals prioritize their tasks, allocate their time efficiently, and avoid wasting time on unimportant activities. It is essential to give specific blocks of time for each job, allowing enough time for each action and avoiding over-commitment.

2. **Use time-tracking tools:** They can help individuals monitor their time usage, identify areas where time is wasted, and make necessary adjustments to their schedule. This can help individuals optimize their time and increase productivity.

3. **Prioritize tasks:** Prioritizing tasks based on their importance and urgency can help individuals focus their time and energy on the most critical activities. This involves determining which tasks are most important and concentrating on completing them before moving on to less urgent tasks.

4. **Learn to say no:** Saying no to activities or commitments that do not align with one's goals or

priorities can help individuals avoid overcommitting their time and energy. It is essential to assess the value of each request and to say no when necessary to prevent spreading oneself too thin.

5. **Break down large tasks:** Breaking down large tasks into more minor, manageable chunks can help individuals avoid feeling overwhelmed and progress toward their goals. This involves breaking an enormous task into smaller, achievable steps and focusing on completing each degree before moving on to the next.

6. **Avoid multitasking:** Multitasking can lead to decreased productivity and increased stress. It is better to focus on completing one task at a time, giving it one's full attention and energy, and moving on to the next task once it is complete.

7. **Use a productivity system:** A productivity system, such as the Pomodoro technique, can help individuals focus on their work and increase productivity. This technique involves working for a set period, usually 25 minutes, and then taking a short break before the next work period begins.

Effective time management can lead to several advantages, including increased productivity, reduced stress, improved work-life balance, a greater sense of accomplishment, and more free time.

When individuals manage their time effectively, they can prioritize their tasks and avoid wasting time on unimportant activities. This leads to increased productivity and can help individuals accomplish more in less time. Effective time management can also help individuals reduce stress by allowing them to stay on top of their commitments and deadlines. When individuals clearly understand what they need to accomplish and when they can avoid feeling overwhelmed and stressed.

Furthermore, effective time management can help individuals better balance their work and personal life, leading to improved relationships, increased happiness, and better overall well-being. When individuals promptly achieve their goals and objectives, they experience a greater sense of accomplishment, boosting self-confidence and motivation. Effective time management can also help individuals make the most of their available time, allowing them to complete their tasks efficiently and freeing up time for other activities, such as spending time with family and friends or pursuing hobbies.

Effective time management gives individuals several advantages that lead to a more fulfilling and enjoyable life. By implementing effective time management strategies, individuals can prioritize their tasks, achieve their goals promptly, and make the most of their available time.

Effective time management has several advantages that can help individuals promptly achieve their goals and objectives. However, it is also essential to consider the potential disadvantages of effective time management strategies.

One potential disadvantage is over-planning, which can lead to rigidity and inflexibility. Individuals who focus too much on planning and organizing their time may miss opportunities or become less creative.

Another potential disadvantage is overworking. Effective time management can sometimes lead to individuals working too much and neglecting their personal life or health. Therefore, finding a balance between work and personal life is essential to avoid burnout and other negative consequences.

Procrastination is another potential disadvantage of effective time management. Paradoxically, individuals focused on managing their time effectively can sometimes become more prone to procrastination. This can occur when individuals set unrealistic goals or need to prioritize tasks more effectively.

Unforeseen events can also disrupt effective time management strategies. While planning and organizing can help individuals manage their time effectively, unexpected events can still disrupt their plans. Being flexible and adaptable in such situations is essential to stay relaxed.

Finally, effective time management can lead to increased pressure to meet deadlines and achieve goals promptly. This can lead to increased stress and anxiety if individuals do not learn to manage these pressures effectively.

Effective time management can have potential disadvantages, including over-planning, overworking, procrastination, unforeseen events, and increased pressure. However, by being aware of these potential downsides, individuals can learn to manage their time effectively while avoiding these negative consequences. It is essential to balance productivity and personal well-being and be adaptable and flexible when unforeseen events occur.

When it comes to managing personal time effectively, there are several practical tips that individuals can follow:

Set clear goals and priorities: Before individuals can effectively manage their time, they must identify their goals and priorities. Individuals can prioritize their tasks and activities by setting clear and achievable goals.

Create a schedule: A schedule can help individuals manage their time effectively by providing a clear structure for their day. By scheduling tasks and activities in advance, individuals can avoid wasting time and ensure they use their time effectively.

Use a planner: A planner can help individuals stay organized and on track with their tasks and activities. By writing down important dates and deadlines, individuals can avoid forgetting essential duties and plan their time accordingly.

Minimize distractions: Distractions can be a significant obstacle to effective time management. To minimize distractions, individuals should turn off their phones, email, and other notifications during designated work times.

Take breaks: Taking breaks can improve productivity by allowing individuals to recharge and refocus. Individuals can maintain their energy and avoid burnout by taking regular intervals throughout the day.

Learn to say no: Learning to say no can be difficult, but it is an essential skill for effective time management. Individuals can free up time for more critical priorities by saying no to nonessential tasks and activities.

Delegate tasks: Delegating tasks can help individuals manage their time more effectively by allowing them to focus on their most important priorities. By delegating tasks to others, individuals can avoid feeling overwhelmed and ensure that all tasks are completed on time.

By following these practical tips, you can better manage your time and achieve your goals promptly and efficiently.

Effective time management is essential for achieving goals, reducing stress, and improving overall well-being. Strategies for better time management include creating a schedule, using time-tracking tools, prioritizing tasks, and learning to say no. While effective time management can lead to many advantages, avoiding becoming too rigid and allowing for rest and relaxation is essential. By incorporating practical advice such as developing a routine, breaking tasks into manageable chunks, taking breaks, and evaluating progress, individuals can improve their time management skills and enjoy the benefits of a more fulfilling and productive life.

Organize To Reduce Stress

Organizing yourself can be a powerful way to reduce stress and increase productivity. Here are some tips on how to get organized and manage stress:

Prioritize your tasks.

Prioritizing your tasks is an essential step in organizing yourself and reducing stress. Here are some tips on how to prioritize your tasks effectively:

Identify urgent tasks.

Start by identifying tasks that are urgent and require immediate attention. These tasks are typically time-sensitive and have a deadline that must be met. Prioritizing critical tasks ensures you can meet important deadlines and prevent last-minute rushing.

Consider importance.

After identifying urgent tasks, consider the importance of each lesson. This involves assessing the impact of each task on your goals, projects, and overall productivity. Prioritizing important tasks ensures you can focus on the most meaningful and valuable work.

Determine the level of effort.

Once you've identified urgent and essential tasks, consider the effort required for each job. Some studies may require more time and effort than others. Prioritizing tasks based on your activity level can help you allocate your time and resources more effectively.

Break down larger tasks.

If you have more significant tasks that seem overwhelming, consider breaking them down into smaller, more manageable steps. This will make it easier to tackle each step individually and prevent you from feeling overwhelmed by the task.

Reassess regularly.

Priorities can shift over time, so it's essential to reassess your task list regularly. This allows you to adjust your preferences based on changing circumstances and prevent essential tasks from falling through the cracks.

By prioritizing your tasks effectively, you can focus your time and energy on the most critical and valuable work, which can help you reduce stress and increase productivity.

Create a schedule.

Creating a schedule is a powerful tool for managing stress and increasing productivity.

Here are some tips on how to create an effective schedule:

Use a calendar or planner.

The first step in creating a schedule is to use a calendar or planner to keep track of your tasks and appointments. Next, choose a format that works best for you: a physical planner or an electronic calendar.

Block out time for important tasks.

Once you've identified your essential tasks, block time on your calendar to work on them. Be realistic about how much time each task will take and allocate enough time to complete each job thoroughly.

Prioritize your most important tasks.

When creating your schedule, prioritize your most important tasks by scheduling them during your most productive hours. This can help ensure you can focus on your most important work when your energy and concentration levels are high.

Schedule breaks

It's important to schedule breaks throughout your day to prevent burnout and maintain your focus. So, block out time on your holiday schedule, and use this time to recharge, stretch, or take a walk.

Avoid multitasking.

While tackling multiple tasks at once may be tempting, multitasking can decrease productivity and increase stress. Instead, focus on one task at a time and give it your full attention.

Be flexible.

It's essential to be flexible and adaptable when creating your schedule. Unexpected events or tasks may arise, so make sure to build some flexibility to accommodate these changes.

Review and adjust your schedule regularly.

Finally, review and adjust your schedule regularly to ensure it's still working for you. Reassess your priorities and adjust your plan as needed to ensure that you can stay on track and meet your goals.

Creating a schedule that works for you allows you to manage your time more effectively, reduce stress, and increase productivity. Remember to be flexible and adaptable, build in breaks and prioritize your most important work.

Use a planner or calendar.

A planner or calendar is a powerful tool for managing stress and increasing productivity.

Choose a planner or calendar that works for you.

Many different types of planners and calendars are available, from physical planners to digital calendars. Choose a format that works best for you and fits your lifestyle and preferences.

Keep your planner or calendar up to date.

Keep your planner or calendar up to date with your appointments, meetings, and deadlines. This will help you stay on track and prevent you from missing important events or tasks.

Use color coding or symbols to organize your schedule.

Color coding or using characters can be a helpful way to organize your schedule and make it easier to read and understand. For example, you might use a different color for work-related, personal, or social events.

Block out time for important tasks.

When creating your schedule, block out time for your most important tasks. This will help you prioritize your work and ensure that you can focus on your most important tasks during your most productive hours.

Be realistic about your time.

When scheduling tasks or appointments, be realistic about your needed time. This will help you avoid overbooking yourself and feeling stressed or overwhelmed.

Use reminders to stay on track.

Many digital calendars and planners offer reminder features that can help you stay on track with your schedule. For example, use reminders to alert you when a deadline is approaching or it's time to start a new task.

Review your planner or calendar regularly.

Finally, review your planner or calendar regularly to ensure it's still working for you. Then, adjust as needed to ensure that you can stay on track and manage your time effectively.

Using a planner or calendar effectively allows you to manage your time more efficiently, reduce stress, and increase productivity. Remember to keep your planner or calendar up to date, be realistic about your time, and use reminders to stay on track.

Declutter your spaces.

Decluttering your space can be a powerful way to reduce stress and increase productivity.

Start small.

When decluttering your space, start with a small area, such as a desk or a drawer. This can help prevent you from feeling overwhelmed and make the process more manageable.

Create designated spaces for each item.

Create designated spaces for each item in your area. This will help you keep track of your belongings and prevent clutter from accumulating. Make sure to put things back in their designated spaces after using them.

Get rid of anything that doesn't serve a purpose or bring you joy.

As you declutter, eliminate anything that doesn't serve a purpose or bring you joy. This can include old papers, broken items, or clothes that no longer fit. Decluttering can be an excellent opportunity to simplify your life and create space for things that bring you happiness and fulfillment.

Use storage solutions.

Using storage solutions, such as shelves or storage bins, can help you keep your space organized and prevent clutter from accumulating. Make sure to label your storage solutions to quickly find what you need.

Regularly reassess your space.

Make decluttering a regular habit by reassessing your space regularly. Set aside time each month to go through your belongings and eliminate anything that no longer serves a purpose or brings you joy.

Avoid overloading your space.

Finally, make sure to avoid overloading your space with too many belongings. This can lead to feelings of overwhelm and stressed. Instead, focus on keeping your area straightforward and streamlined.

By decluttering your space, you can create a more peaceful and organized environment that can help reduce stress and increase productivity. Remember to start small, create designated areas for each item, and regularly reassess your space to prevent clutter from accumulating.

Practice Time Management

Effective time management can help you stay focused and reduce stress.

Identify your priorities.

Start by identifying your priorities, both in your personal and professional life. This can help you focus on the most essential tasks and prevent you from feeling overwhelmed by a long to-do list.

Set realistic goals.

When setting goals, make sure they are realistic and achievable. This will help you avoid feeling discouraged or overwhelmed by unrealistic expectations.

Break down larger tasks.

If you have more significant tasks that seem overwhelming, consider breaking them down into smaller, more manageable steps. This will make it easier to tackle each step individually and prevent you from feeling overwhelmed by the task.

Use a time tracker.

A time tracker can help you identify how you're spending your time and where to improve. Use a tool like Toggl or Rescue Time to track your time and identify areas where you can adjust.

Prioritize your tasks.

List your tasks and prioritize them according to their importance and deadline. This will help you focus on what needs to be done first and prevent you from feeling overwhelmed by a long to-do list.

Use the Pomodoro Technique

The Pomodoro Technique is a time management method that involves working in focused intervals followed by short breaks. This can help you manage your time more effectively and avoid burnout.

Avoid distractions.

Limit distractions like social media and email during work intervals to help you stay focused. You can also use tools like Freedom or Self-control to block distracting websites during work intervals.

Take breaks.

Make sure to take regular breaks throughout your day to prevent burnout and maintain your focus. This can help you stay energized and productive throughout the day

By practicing effective time management, you can reduce stress and increase productivity. Remember to set realistic goals, prioritize your tasks, and avoid distractions. As a result, you can create a more peaceful and productive life by managing your time effectively.

Set Boundaries

Setting boundaries is essential in managing stress and maintaining a healthy work-life balance.

Identify your priorities.

Start by identifying your priorities and what's most important to you. This can help you set boundaries that align with your values and goals.

Communicate your boundaries clearly.

Make sure to communicate your boundaries clear to others. This can include setting limits on your availability for work or social engagements or asking others to respect your need for downtime.

Say "no" when necessary.

It's okay to say "no" to requests or invitations that don't align with your priorities or boundaries. This can help you avoid overcommitting yourself and feeling overwhelmed.

Avoid overworking.

Set boundaries around your work schedule and avoid overworking. Take breaks throughout the day and prioritize your mental and physical health.

Take care of your own needs.

Make sure to prioritize your own needs and take care of yourself. This can include setting aside time for self-care activities like exercise, meditation, or reading.

Manage technology use.

Set boundaries around your use of technology, such as turning off notifications during certain times of the day or avoiding social media during work hours.

Learn to delegate.

If you're feeling overwhelmed, consider delegating tasks to others who can help. This can free up your time and allow you to focus on tasks that align with your priorities.

Regularly reassess your boundaries.

Make sure to regularly reassess your boundaries to ensure that they're still working for you. Your priorities and needs may change over time, so adjusting your limits is essential.

By setting boundaries, you can manage your time and energy more effectively, reduce stress, and maintain a healthy work-life balance. Remember to communicate your boundaries clearly, say "no" when necessary, and prioritize your needs. Setting and respecting your boundaries can create a more peaceful and fulfilling life.

How to improve your productivity

Improving productivity is an essential aspect of achieving personal and professional success. It involves carefully examining your current habits, setting well-defined goals, and employing strategies tailored to your circumstances. To effectively boost your productivity, consider implementing the following suggestions.

Begin by setting clear goals for both short-term and long-term objectives. Having a sense of direction allows you to maintain focus and measure your progress over time. Once you have established your goals, break them into smaller, more manageable tasks. This will make it easier to tackle complex projects without feeling overwhelmed.

Prioritizing tasks is crucial for managing your time effectively. To ensure that you dedicate your energy to the most critical missions, determine which ones should be completed first. One helpful method for this is the Eisenhower Matrix, which categorizes tasks based on urgency and importance. As a result, you can allocate your time and resources more efficiently by distinguishing between tasks that require immediate attention and those that can be deferred.

Creating a schedule is another essential component of improving productivity. Establish a daily routine that includes designated time slots for each task. This will help you maintain a consistent workflow and make it easier to track your progress. Be sure to adhere to your schedule as closely as possible, but also allow for some flexibility in case unexpected challenges or opportunities arise.

Minimizing distractions is critical to maintaining focus and staying on task. First, identify familiar sources of distraction, such as social media, unnecessary notifications, or background noise, and take steps to eliminate or reduce them. For instance, consider setting your devices to "Do Not Disturb" mode during work hours or using noise-canceling headphones to block out distractions in your environment.

Productivity tools and apps can also be highly beneficial in helping you stay organized, manage your time, and monitor your progress. Numerous task management applications, calendars, and timers can be tailored to suit your specific needs. Experiment with different tools to find the ones that work best for you.

Dividing large tasks into smaller parts can help prevent feeling overwhelmed and make complex projects more approachable. In addition, breaking tasks into more manageable sub-tasks allows you to track your progress more quickly and celebrate small victories.

Taking regular breaks is essential for maintaining your focus and energy levels. In addition, short breaks can help refresh your mind and stave off burnout. One popular time management technique is the Pomodoro Technique, which involves working for 25 minutes and a 5-minute break. This cycle is repeated throughout the workday, providing a structured balance between focused work and restorative breaks.

Delegating tasks when possible is another valuable strategy for improving productivity. By entrusting specific tasks to others, you can free up time and mental bandwidth to focus on your most important responsibilities. Recognize when delegation is appropriate, and don't hesitate to ask for help when needed.

Cultivating good habits can have a significant impact on your overall productivity. For example, maintain a clean and organized workspace, get adequate sleep, eat well, and exercise regularly.

These habits will boost your productivity and contribute to your overall well-being.

Finally, be open to learning and adapting as you continue your productivity journey. Stay receptive to new ideas and techniques that help you work more efficiently. Regularly assess your progress and adjust your strategies as needed. Remember that everyone's path to productivity is unique, so finding the best approaches for you is essential.

How to Create a Positive Mindset

Mindset refers to the collection of beliefs, attitudes, and thoughts that shape how we perceive ourselves, our abilities, and the world around us. It is the lens through which we view our experiences and influences how we respond to challenges and setbacks. A positive mindset can help us achieve our goals, overcome obstacles, and live a fulfilling life.

Training our mindset every day is essential because our philosophy is not fixed but rather something that can be developed and strengthened over time. We can cultivate a more positive and resilient outlook by actively working on our perspective.

Training our mindset daily involves intentionally focusing on positive thoughts, beliefs, and attitudes. It consists in challenging negative self-talk and limiting beliefs and replacing them with positive affirmations and constructive ideas. It also involves practicing mindfulness and gratitude to help us stay present and appreciate the good things in our lives.

Here are some reasons why it's essential to train our mindset every day:

Improves Resilience

A positive mindset can help us bounce back from setbacks and challenges more easily. By training our philosophy to focus on the positive and believe in our abilities, we can become more resilient and better equipped to handle stress and adversity.

Boosts Confidence

A positive mindset can help to boost our confidence and self-esteem. Focusing on our strengths and accomplishments can build a more positive self-image and make us feel more confident in our abilities.

Increases Productivity

A positive mindset can increase productivity by reducing distractions and helping us to stay focused on our goals. By training our philosophy to focus on positive thoughts and beliefs, we can become more motivated and driven to achieve our goals.

Enhances Relationships

A positive mindset can also enhance our relationships with others. By practicing empathy, kindness, and gratitude, we can strengthen our connections with others and build more positive and fulfilling relationships.

Promotes Overall Well-Being

A positive mindset can have a positive impact on our overall well-being. By reducing stress and increasing feelings of happiness and contentment, we can improve our physical and mental health and enjoy a more fulfilling life.

In summary, mindset is the collection of beliefs, attitudes, and thoughts that shape how we perceive ourselves and the world around us. Therefore, we must train our mindset daily by focusing on positive thoughts, beliefs, and attitudes, challenging negative self-talk, and limiting beliefs, and practicing mindfulness and gratitude. By cultivating a positive and resilient mindset, we can improve our overall well-being and live a more fulfilling life.

Cultivating Gratitude and Appreciation

Cultivating gratitude and appreciation is an essential aspect of creating a positive mindset. It involves developing an attitude of gratitude, which can help to shift our focus from the negative aspects of life to the positive ones. Gratitude is not just a fleeting feeling of thankfulness but rather an intentional and deliberate practice that can profoundly impact our well-being.

Gratitude has been linked to numerous benefits, including improved mental health, greater happiness and life satisfaction, stronger relationships, and enhanced physical health. It can also help reduce stress and anxiety, boost self-esteem, and increase resilience and optimism. Here are some tips for cultivating gratitude and appreciation in your life:

Keep a Gratitude Journal

One of the most effective ways to cultivate gratitude is to keep a gratitude journal. This involves taking a few minutes each day to reflect on the things you are grateful for and writing them down. You can do this first thing in the morning or just before bed. The important thing is to be consistent and make it a habit.

When writing in your gratitude journal, be specific about what you are grateful for. Don't just say you are thankful for your family, for example. Instead, write about a particular moment or interaction with your family that made you feel grateful. This will help to deepen your sense of gratitude and appreciation.

Practice Mindfulness

Mindfulness is being fully present now, without judgment or distraction. Practicing mindfulness can help you to become more aware of the good things in your life and appreciate them more fully. Mindfulness can be practiced in many ways, such as meditation, deep breathing, or simply paying attention to your surroundings.

To practice mindfulness, find a quiet place where you won't be interrupted. Sit comfortably with your eyes closed and focus on your breath. Notice the sensations of your breath as it enters and leaves your body. If your mind wanders, gently bring your attention back to your breath. You can practice mindfulness for a few minutes daily or more extended periods if you have more time.

Express Gratitude to Others

Expressing gratitude to others is another effective way to cultivate gratitude and appreciation. When you express gratitude to others, you not only make them feel good, but you also strengthen your own sense of gratitude and appreciation.

There are many ways to express gratitude to others. You can say thank you, write a thank-you note or email, or simply tell someone how much you appreciate them. Be specific about what you are grateful for and how it has impacted you. This will make your expression of gratitude more meaningful and impactful.

Reframe Negative Experiences

Negative experiences can be challenging but reframing them in a more positive light can help cultivate gratitude and appreciation. When something negative happens, try to find the silver lining. Ask yourself what you learned from the experience or what good came out of it.

For example, if you lose your job, you might feel angry or upset at first. But suppose you reframe the experience as an opportunity to find a better job or pursue a new career path. In that case, you can find reasons to be grateful for the occasion. Moreover, by reframing negative experiences, you can train your mind to focus on the positive and become more resilient in facing challenges.

Focus on Abundance

Finally, focusing on abundance can help you to cultivate gratitude and appreciation. Instead of thinking about what you lack or wish you had, focus on what you do have. Count your blessings and appreciate the abundance in your life. This can include things like your health, relationships, home, job, and hobbies.

When you focus on abundance, you shift your mindset from one of scarcity to one of abundance. You begin to see the good things in your life as gifts to be appreciated rather than as things you owe or take for granted. This can help you to feel more content and satisfied with your life.

To focus on abundance, list the things you are grateful for in your life. Be as specific as possible and include things you might take for granted. Then, take a moment to appreciate each item on your list. You can even say a quick thank-you or offer a prayer of gratitude for each item.

By cultivating gratitude and appreciation, you can create a more positive mindset focused on the good things in your life. This can help you feel happier, more content, and more resilient in facing challenges. Try incorporating these tips into your daily routine and see how they can help cultivate gratitude and appreciation.

Building Resilience and Emotional Intelligence

Building resilience and emotional intelligence is essential to creating a positive mindset. Strength refers to our ability to bounce back from challenges and setbacks. In contrast, emotional intelligence refers to our ability to recognize, understand, and manage our emotions and those of others. These skills can help us better cope with stress, overcome obstacles, and lead more fulfilling lives.

Here are some tips for building resilience and emotional intelligence:

Practice Self-Care

Self-care is essential for building resilience and emotional intelligence. This involves taking care of your physical, mental, and emotional health. Make time for exercise, healthy eating, and restful sleep. Practice mindfulness and relaxation techniques such as meditation, yoga, or deep breathing. Take breaks when needed and prioritize activities that bring you joy and fulfillment.

Build a Support System

Having a solid support system can help to build resilience and emotional intelligence. This can include family, friends, colleagues, or a therapist. It's essential to have people in your life who you can turn to for support and guidance during challenging times. In addition, building positive relationships can boost your emotional intelligence by providing opportunities to practice empathy and communication skills.

Learn from Mistakes

Mistakes and failures are an inevitable part of life, but they can also be valuable learning experiences. Instead of dwelling on your mistakes or beating yourself up for them, try to learn from them. Ask yourself what you can do differently next time and what lessons you can take from the experience. This can help you to become more resilient and better equipped to handle future challenges.

Develop Emotional Awareness

Emotional awareness is recognizing and understanding your emotions and those of others. This is an essential aspect of emotional intelligence and can help you to better navigate social interactions and build stronger relationships. To develop emotional awareness, practice tuning in and labeling your emotions. You can also practice active listening and empathy with others to better understand their feelings.

Practice Mindfulness

Mindfulness is a powerful tool for building resilience and emotional intelligence. By practicing mindfulness, you can become more aware of your thoughts, feelings, and physical sensations. This can help you better regulate your emotions and respond to challenges more calmly and effectively. To practice mindfulness, focus on the present moment without judgment or distraction. You can do this through meditation, deep breathing, or simply paying attention to your surroundings.

By practicing these tips for building resilience and emotional intelligence, you can become more adept at handling stress, overcoming obstacles, and leading a more fulfilling life. Of course, these skills take time and practice to develop. Still, you can cultivate a more positive and resilient mindset with consistency and dedication.

Reframing Negative Thoughts and Beliefs

Reframing negative thoughts and beliefs is essential to creating a positive mindset. Negative thoughts and ideas can lead to feelings of anxiety, depression, and low self-esteem, making it difficult to live a fulfilling life. Reframing these thoughts and beliefs can help to shift your mindset from one of negativity to one of positivity and possibility.

Here are some tips for reframing negative thoughts and beliefs:

Identify Negative Thoughts and Beliefs

The first step in reframing negative thoughts and beliefs is to identify them. Negative thoughts and ideas can be automatic and may occur without realizing them. Pay attention to your inner dialogue and notice when you engage in negative self-talk or when negative beliefs arise.

Write down these negative thoughts and beliefs as they come up. Being aware of them can help you challenge and reframe them in a more positive light.

Challenge Negative Thoughts and Beliefs

Once you have identified your negative thoughts and beliefs, challenge them. First, ask yourself whether they are based on reality, assumptions, or interpretations. Next, consider the evidence that supports or contradicts the negative thought or belief.

For example, if you believe you are not good enough, challenge this belief by asking yourself if there is any evidence to support this belief. Is it based on past experiences, or is it just a self-imposed belief? Look for evidence contradicting this belief, such as compliments from others or accomplishments you have achieved.

Reframe Negative Thoughts and Beliefs

After challenging negative thoughts and beliefs, it's time to reframe them in a more positive light. This involves finding alternative and more positive interpretations of the situation. Instead of thinking negatively, reframe the situation more positively and constructively.

For example, if you failed a test and think, "I'm so stupid," reframe this thought by thinking, "I didn't do as well as I wanted, but I can learn from my mistakes and do better next time."

Practice Positive Self-Talk

Positive self-talk involves using affirming and empowering language to boost your self-esteem and confidence. This can help to reframe negative thoughts and beliefs by replacing them with positive and empowering ones. When you engage in negative self-talk, try reframing your thoughts in a more positive light.

For example, instead of saying, "I can't do this," say, "I am capable and resilient." Repeat positive affirmations to yourself throughout the day to reinforce positive thinking and reframe negative thoughts and beliefs.

Practice Gratitude

Practicing gratitude can also help to reframe negative thoughts and beliefs. By focusing on the positive aspects of your life, you can shift your mindset from negativity to positivity and appreciation. Make a daily habit of writing down three things you are grateful for. These can be small or big things, but focusing on the positive can help reframe negative thoughts and beliefs.

By practicing these tips for reframing negative thoughts and beliefs, you can develop a more positive and resilient mindset. Of course, this takes practice and dedication. Still, you can transform your mood and live a more fulfilling life by challenging negative thoughts and ideas and reframing them positively.

Replace negative thoughts with positive ones.

Negative thoughts can powerfully impact our mood, behavior, and overall outlook. They can lead to feelings of anxiety, depression, and low self-esteem, making it difficult to achieve our goals and live a fulfilling life. However, it is possible to replace negative thoughts with positive ones through various creative and effective strategies. Here are some tips to help you replace negative thoughts with positive ones:

Challenge Negative Thoughts

Challenging negative thoughts is the first step in replacing them with positive ones. Identify negative thoughts as they arise and ask yourself if they are based on reality, assumptions, or interpretations. Next, challenge the evidence supporting negative thoughts and consider alternative, more positive explanations.

For example, if you have a negative thought that says, "I'm not good enough," challenge this thought by asking yourself if it's true. Is it based on facts or just a feeling? Then, look for evidence contradicting this thought, such as positive feedback from others or past successes.

Reframe Negative Thoughts

Reframing negative thoughts involves replacing them with positive ones. First, identify negative thoughts and find alternative and optimistic interpretations of the situation. Then, instead of thinking negatively, reframe the situation more positively and constructively.

For example, if you have a negative thought that says, "I'll never be able to do this," reframe this thought by thinking, "I may not be able to do it right now, but I can learn and improve."

Use Positive Affirmations

Positive affirmations are statements you repeat to yourself that help reinforce positive thinking and reframe negative thoughts. They can be as simple as "I am strong and capable" or "I can handle anything that comes my way." Repeat positive affirmations to yourself throughout the day to reinforce positive thinking and replace negative thoughts.

Visualize Positive Outcomes

Visualizing positive outcomes can replace negative thoughts with positive ones. Imagine yourself achieving your goals and feeling happy and fulfilled. Visualize yourself in a positive and successful light and focus on the positive emotions that come with it. By visualizing positive outcomes, you can replace negative thoughts with positive ones and feel more confident and empowered.

Surround Yourself with Positive People

Surrounding yourself with positive people can also help to replace negative thoughts with positive ones. Seek out people who are positive, supportive, and uplifting. Avoid people who are negative, critical, and pessimistic. By surrounding yourself with positive people, you can reinforce positive thinking and replace negative thoughts with positive ones.

Practice Mindfulness

Mindfulness is being fully present now, without judgment or distraction. By practicing mindfulness, you can become more aware of your thoughts and emotions and learn to observe them without judgment. This can help you replace negative thoughts with positive ones by noticing when negative thoughts arise and reframing them in a more positive light.

In summary, many creative and effective ways exist to replace negative thoughts with positive ones. You can cultivate a more positive and resilient mindset by challenging negative thoughts, reframing them in a more positive light, using positive affirmations, visualizing positive outcomes, practicing gratitude, surrounding yourself with positive people, and practicing mindfulness. With practice and dedication, you can replace negative thoughts with positive ones and live a more fulfilling life.

Conclusion

Overthinking can be a debilitating and exhausting habit that can lead to feelings of anxiety, stress, and a lack of fulfillment in life. However, with the right strategies and mindset, it is possible to break free from this pattern of overthinking and live a more fulfilling life.

This book explored three critical strategies for creating a positive mindset and overcoming overthinking: cultivating gratitude and appreciation, building resilience and emotional intelligence, and reframing negative thoughts and beliefs. By applying these strategies in your daily life, you can gradually develop a new conception of your personality and life.

Cultivating gratitude and appreciation involves focusing on the positive aspects of your life and learning to appreciate them. By focusing on what you have rather than your lack, you can cultivate a more positive and content mindset.

Building resilience and emotional intelligence involves developing the skills and strategies to cope with challenges and setbacks. By taking care of your physical, mental, and emotional health, building a solid support system, learning from mistakes, practicing positive self-talk, developing emotional awareness, and practicing mindfulness, you can become more resilient and better equipped to handle stress and adversity.

Reframing negative thoughts and beliefs involves challenging negative self-talk, limiting beliefs, and replacing them with positive affirmations and constructive ideas. You can cultivate a more positive and resilient mindset by focusing on the positive, reframing negative thoughts, and practicing gratitude.

It's important to remember that changing your mindset takes time and effort. It's not something that happens overnight but rather a gradual process of building new habits and ways of thinking. So be patient with yourself and celebrate your progress along the way.

By reading and applying the advice in this book, you can gradually develop a new conception of your personality and life. You can learn to overcome overthinking and cultivate a more positive and fulfilling mindset. Remember to be kind to yourself, take things one step at a time, and celebrate your progress. With dedication and perseverance, you can break free from overthinking and live a more fulfilling life.

In conclusion, the strategies and tips outlined in this book can help you to overcome overthinking, cultivate a positive mindset, and maintain a sense of calm and focus on your daily life. However, it's important to remember that changing your mindset and habits takes time and effort. It's not something that happens overnight but rather a gradual process of building new habits and ways of thinking.

The key to success is a daily practice, determination, and the belief that you can change your life. Committing to a daily routine, staying determined, and believing that you can achieve your goals can create profound changes in your life and how you perceive reality.

Remember to be kind to yourself, celebrate your progress, and keep moving forward. With dedication and perseverance, you can overcome overthinking, cultivate a positive mindset, and maintain a sense of calm and focus on your daily life. Your efforts will benefit yourself and those around you as you become more positive, resilient, and compassionate. So, take the first step today and begin your journey towards a happier, more fulfilling life.

Support my Work

If you enjoyed the contents of this book and want to help me in a simple, accessible, and fast way, I warmly invite you to leave an honest review directly on the Amazon product page. That way, other people looking for vegetarian recipes and other vegetarian diet-related content will find my book and all my work. To do this, use the camera on your smartphone to scan the QR code or click on this link if you have the reader in the digital version.

Thank you, Rudolf.

Printed in Great Britain
by Amazon